CEDAR MILL COMM LIBRARY
D
IN
ARY

D0175738

planting gardens in graves II

r.h. Sin

Andrews McMeel
PUBLISHING®

other books by r.h. Sin

Whiskey Words & a Shovel

Whiskey Words & a Shovel II

Whiskey Words & a Shovel III

Rest in the Mourning

A Beautiful Composition of Broken

Algedonic

She Felt Like Feeling Nothing

September.

i stayed

but love left

silent echoes.

broken hearts scream
the sound of silence

who you truly are.

you'll make it

you always do

you're the girl

who tames

the flames

you're the girl

who always survives

filled with fear.

the fear of losing others
has caused me to walk away

a smothered mind.

so much sadness

in her silence

so many questions

on her mind

self-inflicted.

we get hurt

by our own expectations

broken joy.

look at all
the pretty girls
with the broken smiles

death by a dozen.

we were like roses
kept alive for the moment
left to die in the end

search in solitude.

i waited

you never showed

i tried

without your effort

i left

without regret

i'll be fine

without you

girl sitting alone.

lips the color of blood

hair tangled down

to the roots

peace has forgotten

your name

love has become

a stranger

torn mentally.

was it real

will you remember me

do you miss me yet

i ask questions

i know the answers to

i overthink myself

into a mood

that robs me of my happiness

i am at my worst

with you on my mind

rotten beneath.

sitting on the realization

that you were never good

and this was never love

like a beautiful peach

rotten on the inside

almost to the bottom.

i held my own hand

weak, tired

almost lifeless

ready to leave

it all behind

i leaped into

the darkness

and caught myself

i became my own hero

and as cliché as it may sound

i saved my own soul

most unfortunate.

the prettiest souls
have the greatest stories
of heartache

what i know.

forever is always
shorter than we expect

cutting board.

with lies as sharp as knives
they'll cut you open
then give you a half-ass apology
to cover your wounds

soul sought.

funny
i couldn't see a thing
until i closed my eyes
my soul saw you
for who you truly were

assist.

it takes two

to save a relationship

you can't continue

to do this

by yourself

prioritize.

chase success

not him

choose yourself

not him

peak.

put your heart
on top of a mountain
the men who don't
deserve you
don't have the strength
to reach it

of gold.

the women they claim

are broken

hold a love within

their hearts

the value of gold

conclusion.

she survived you
tired from fighting
she moved forward
she finally let go

observations.

she's strong enough

to overcome

her weaknesses

the heels.

she walked through hell
in heels wearing a smile
nothing could stop her
nothing could keep her down

angel number 22.

soulmates find themselves

in one another

evermore.

in order to find myself
i had to lose myself
you broke me down
i came back stronger

beside you.

trying to dream
next to you
was a nightmare

heat.

your love
like hell
and i was kissing
the devil

of many.

dating in my generation

has become kissing the lips

of many devils

in search of heaven

on earth

content.

struck ill by overthinking

overwhelming thoughts

assuming the worst

because the worst

always happens

i'm more accustomed

to getting hurt

i am used to being used

i've grown content

with dysfunction

more than none.

most of the men you meet
will have nothing to offer
choose yourself more often
choose a life
without their b.s.

October 25th.

you were never worth
the time i invested

generation denial.

my generation

always dating

but never go on dates

always so in love

while complaining

about the pain

dead alive.

we drag the lifeless bodies

of our relationships

claiming to be in love

ruining ourselves

for people who never truly cared

of layers.

a woman has many layers
dig deeper beyond the surface
of what you see

behind bars.

caged behind denial

and confusion

i see my freedom

from behind the bars

surrounding my heart

and deep down i know

love isn't meant

to feel like prison

but my choices made me

your prisoner

my choices keep me here

for me, by me.

for too long

we wait for a love

that can be cultivated

by our own hearts

a love that can be given

to ourselves from ourselves

laid.

you lead with sex
and so it ends
after they cum

of nothingness.

you filled me up
with emptiness
and despair

of anxiety.

my anxiety has become

the death of my peace

unwillingly

i dive into the madness

of my mind

and the pain within my soul

eagerness.

sometimes i'm eager

to feel the warmth of love

even though i've grown

more familiar

with the cold hands of heartache

conceal.

the more i suffer

the bigger my smile

appearing whole to others

while broken within

concluded.

i've come to this realization
after weeks of mourning us
i needed me a bit more
than you deserved me

November 1st.

broken relationships

like rooms with holes

in the ceiling

leaking lies

betrayal dripping

to the floor as it rains

outside

but soon i'll be moving

relocating my heart

oversight.

it turned out
you were a mistake
not a soulmate

painful quest.

the heart is stubborn

searching for dedication

and love

in the person who broke it

of torment.

memories are just

painful daydreams

nightmares for the restless

visions of ghosts

a continuous haunt

troubles.

we have loved

more than we've been loved

and that is the problem

variations.

the kind of love you accept
depends on how much
you love yourself

self, all knowing.

never let them
dictate your value
know thyself completely

blank pages.

i began making a list
of all the benefits
of loving you
and the page remained blank

numbed.

you could chill
a bottle of moscato
with her heart

to the brim.

sometimes all a woman needs
is a viewing of her favorite show
with a glass of wine in her hand
it's that simple

soaked in fall.

she was wet enough
to drown my sorrows
my pain

ups and downs.

every relationship and or marriage
has its ups and downs but in no way
is that an excuse to stay
with someone who chooses
to mistreat you
the fact that no one is perfect
doesn't serve as an excuse
to hold on to someone
who continues to break your heart
or causes you to question
your relationship
you can keep fighting but your fight
means nothing
if they're not fighting for you
as well

before.

i was starving

in the silence

of your neglect

make flames.

the world is cold
burn bridges to keep warm

wrong fight.

it's fucked up

because we find ourselves

fighting for those

who would rather

fight against us

rarity.

she will always be
some sort of rare occurrence
that you couldn't appreciate
and no matter how much
time passes
she'll be the girl
you will never forget

in ruins.

we ruin every inch
of ourselves
by overthinking

in my silence.

i see everything

i know so much

but i don't say anything

cold walls.

i want to love
but my heart feels
like winter and i'm tired
of being hurt

hear me.

listen

i will no longer

feel guilty

for choosing myself

at your convenience.

you only love me
when it's convenient
for you
my name forgotten
when my presence
isn't needed

keep hope.

i hope you find someone
who still loves you
even when they're upset

coldest.

numb

my heart

the feel

of winter

you are.

she is anything and everything, always

out loud.

don't hide her
love her out loud

perished.

one day i won't be around
and you will no longer
be able to hurt me

October end.

time and time again

people have continuously

let me down

i have often been subjected

to some sort of emotional

mistreatment or punishment

due to the selfishness

of others

and yet i find myself

pushing the limits

going above and beyond

for the people

who don't love themselves

enough

to appreciate me

my heart is damaged
in a way that i can't describe
with words and any feeling
i've had is gone like silence

in the night
i'm numb
eager to feel more
of nothing
eager to forget
those who have
forgotten about me
this life is painful
my life

nothing hurts more
than doing so much for people
who make you feel
like what you do isn't enough

almost November.

i'm angry because

my time was wasted

i'm cold because

my heart was betrayed

my trust issues come from years

of overtrusting the wrong people

don't judge me for who i am

without understanding

that i loved with everything
within me

that i fought with the idea of
walking away

and none of that mattered

because i've often found myself

giving my all to those

who gave nothing to me

later on that night.

you're just tired
i've watched you grow weak
under the weight of disappointment
i've witnessed you fight
and not be fought for
your heart overflowing but breaking
you're drowning and falling apart
and yet you smile
as if none of this is hurting you
but i feel it
i notice
i understand

midnights are always

the hardest

i struggle to the surface

of my emotions

drowning beneath

the thickness of it all

November 9th 2016.

you're a survivor
and you'll survive this
as well

peace compromised.

i watch you

compromise

your peace of mind

for the chaos of a man

who is incapable

of loving you

and i hope you find

the strength

to walk away

painful, beautiful process.

fuck you for making me

reconsider my self-worth

i lowered my standards

in order to keep you

and now losing you

means gaining my dignity back

you, a rarity.

she's a rare breed of woman

who deserves someone who

will appreciate and love

all the things that most men
overlook

before and after.

he used to look like love
she used to be so happy

master of beasts.

lions bow

at her feet

wolves fear

her strength

in all honesty.

you are not secure in your
relationship
he is not keeping
you safe

trust what you feel.

too often

women are made

to appear crazy

when they make

assumptions

that are true about the men in
their lives

the 15th floor.

and here i stand
surrounded by my own tears
knee deep in my own demons
reaching for the same hand
who pushed me over the edge

too late, soon after.

my heart
a pistol of emotion
that i've turned against myself
causing my own demise
while choosing to love you

darkest days.

i am poetry

written on imaginary lines

the words on crumpled up paper

tossed in the trash

i am poetry

only expressed while in pain

only written down

during bouts of insanity

i am poetry

in search of peace

while the chaos of this world

continues to haunt me

i am poetry . . .

reactionary to pain.

i can hear the blood
rushing through my veins
like cars on highways
my heart begins to crack
under the pressure
of loving you
i am now waist deep
in the flood of everything
we were
and everything we
should've been and usually
i'd try for you
but this time
i'm saving myself

no longer.

i've adapted to the cold
no longer do i shiver
under the falling flakes
of winter
no longer do i break
at the sign of heartache

the after hours.

i've been waiting patiently

for all the things you promised

holding on to every dream you sold
me

drowning in a pool of my own
regret

unable to walk away from you

knowing i should

unable to move on

seemingly accepting the shackles

you placed on my wrists

it hurts but i just sit here

and pretend that it doesn't

my entire body restless

lying here in the dark

trying to find the strength

to leave you behind

love after pain.

my mother would hit me

her way of teaching me discipline

and after every beating

she'd say she loved me

and this is why i associate

love with pain

absent father.

daddy was never there

and so when she became a woman

she tried to fill the void

with men who resembled

the characteristics of her father

unlearning toxic love.

everything i witnessed

as a child who was supposed to be

too young to remember certain things

has molded me into the adult

that i shouldn't be

the screaming and yelling

the tension and resentment

all the things i thought were normal

the same things i was content with

within my own relationships

the drama i accepted

the abuse i didn't mind

trying to find real love

yet not knowing what real love was

it's time to unlearn

the teachings of what i witnessed

in people who were incapable

of loving each other

my parents

an hour until three.

today was bittersweet
the love i shared for you
has gone up in flames
and in this 40-degree weather
i'm now using those flames
to keep me warm
this was never love
but i was fooled
by your desire to waste
my time
this was barely love
but i believed in us
out of fear of loneliness

today was bittersweet
but at least i now know
that your love was a lie

in mourning.

sometimes you have

to mourn your old relationship

to move past it

sometimes you have to cry

to empty yourself of pain

there is peace

in breaking down

there is hope

in cleansing yourself

of a relationship

that caused you pain

3rd day in December.

cheating and deceit

glamorized filth

romanticizing a love

that isn't love

we've become numb

to what hurts

giving others permission

to destroy our hearts

4th day in December.

lowered standards

prevents romance

sincere.

she's going to leave you
for someone like me
and that's when
you'll lose her for life

arms open.

you're tired

and i am rest

you're hurting

and i am relief

you've kept it all in

but i'll be your release

there is freedom in my love

i have no desire to tame you

you're used to doing everything

on your own

and i'm not trying to save you

i just want to be there

next to you, arms open

i'll be ready when you're ready

i'll be here

when you're available

double tap.

we just like things

other people's vacations

children of strangers

cats and puppies

books on shelves

the bare skin of women

in search of validation

through social media

we people watch

from the four walls

of our homes

or the cubicle at the job

that we hate

we're always liking things

we don't love anymore

we're always liking things

we don't live anymore

the girl in photos.

in all honesty
i believe my truth
exists within you
i believe that i'll find
the love that i'm after
behind the walls
of your broken heart
i see beauty in your brokenness
i see value in your existence
and i'm inspired by your strength
you're the type of woman
who deserves what she gives
you're the type of woman
who'd make the reaper
want to live
roses envy you
blooming beneath the sun
staring at photos of you
i'm starting to think
i've found the one

to the reader.

why are you here

what made you pick up this book

who hurt you

what are you truly feeling

as you thumb through these pages

do these words

jump out at you

do these words resonate

with the pain in your heart

i'm here if you need me

i'm here always

you are not a burden

i won't judge you

i'll do my best to understand

i hope you find what you're looking for

Samantha King taught us.

reading *born to love, cursed to feel*

by Samantha King

the sun hidden beneath

the darkness of the night sky

the air is cold

colder than usual

just enough to match my icy heart

we are everything, giving everything

to those who deserve nothing

we are in love with those

incapable of loving us

we are too involved

distracted by those

who don't deserve our attention

i know this now

better late than never

search for kings.

queens searching for a royal love
within a relationship
with men who will never be kings

thank you Samantha.

it was late and you were sleeping
the moon sat outside our window
watching us
staring at me, staring at you
and i can honestly say
that love has never been as true
as us two, lying beside one another

your guy.

your man's desire
to be everything to you
should outweigh
the importance of every other
woman in the world

combative.

look at you
playing the devil's advocate
fighting against me
while fighting for others
offended by the facts
defensive with your views
my opinion drowned out
by your anger
i used to wonder why
you'd rather fight me
but it took me until today
to no longer care

validate.

don't turn this around on me

your need for validation

your insecurities are not mine

and if you owned your faults

as much as you claim to

there would never be a need

to fight so hard to prove to others

that you are who you say you are

no reply.

there's no need

to read your text messages

you're too predictable

for your own good

i know what you'll say

several overly emotional lines

to make yourself appear

to be the victim

and me, the heartless bastard

who forced you to feel this way

by doing nothing

or saying things you didn't agree with

usually i respond

lowering my standards

to argue with you

but this time i'll provide silence

this time, i'll say nothing

unemployment.

love became work

this is why my heart

is unemployed

in time.

time has become my greatest enemy
eating away at the foundation
of my relationship
like termites to wood
the good has been replaced
by forced laughter and fake smiles
the time we made for each other
now spent scrolling up and down
on social media apps
where did the love go . . .

i do, you don't.

without loyalty and truth
without compromise and sacrifice
the ring is just a ring
a symbol of everything
you thought marriage
could've been

in damaged soil.

slowly, losing my desire to love

ever so obvious, the desire to be
left alone

no longer willing to tolerate

the actions of those who are
unwilling

and too immature to respect my
heart

i've placed the responsibility of
loyalty

in dirty hands with bad intent

and malice in their hearts

envy in their eyes

deceit in their soul

i tried sowing seeds of hope

in damaged soil

planting seeds of trust

where they could never grow

slowly, you're losing me

onward.

always saying i'll leave tomorrow
but tomorrow came today
i tried fighting for your love
and now i can no longer stay

on Monday.

the sun goes into hiding

slowly behind the skyscrapers

until the Hudson River

swallows it whole

there is little light left

along with the colors

on the tip of the Empire State
Building

i see people working

across the way

windows like open galleries

depicting a man yelling on the phone

hard at work

and a woman whose face reads

restlessness

a janitor on a lower level

cleaning up the mess

of those too inconsiderate

to even care

me writing this after an argument

with the one i love

and you reading these words

in search of peace

we all have our stories

some big, some small

all important

life, a bad dream.

it almost feels like a bad dream
but i'm awake, living the nightmare
that we created together

backwards.

people aren't who they claim they are
and rarely do they ever become
the person they pretend to be
this is the truth that we struggle
to grasp
and i can always feel myself slipping
back into old habits
falling backwards into a place
i thought i'd left behind
revisiting a relationship
that felt more like a crime scene
my heart outlined in chalk
and you behind the yellow tape
watching me bleed out
yet somehow i believe
the apologies of someone
who refuses to change
their behavior

toward the end.

i think you know it's over
the urge to check their emails
texts and the inbox
of their direct messages
are only precursors
to everything you already know
there's this weird feeling
in your gut
that you haven't been able
to shake
there's this restlessness
when you should be asleep
that keeps you awake
you've known for a while now
but you suppress these things
because the truth is harder
to face
i think you know it's over
you've reached your limit

young me.

when you're young
you think you have so much time
and so you waste it
on people who will mean nothing
in 10 years
yet instead of cultivating
a love that'll last
you entertain relationships
that won't

one line left.

lately i've been walking the line
of insanity
seemingly daring myself
to cross the line of crazy
nearing the edge of losing my mind
and i know that if i break
that barrier
i won't know how
to find my way back

black barrel.

hopefully this whiskey
will quiet the screams
of my demons

not around.

he spends all his time
away from you
and when he comes home
he finds reasons to leave
maybe it's to a friend's house
maybe a trip to the gym
anything to get away
that's more than enough reason
for you not to stay

between the books.

those aisles of books

seem so damn endless

i see a girl reading

born to love, cursed to feel

sitting on the floor

in a floral dress

another young woman

eyeing *whiskey words & a shovel*

while clutching *rest in the mourning*

and i just smile

because there's magic

in the woman who reads

the 13th.

i stopped believing in you
sometime back
before i felt secure
back when you actually
made an effort
and now i'm staring in the mirror
at a face that i don't recognize
once happy because of you
now there's only sadness left
i miss the way we were
i miss the way you used
to treat me
i've been missing the version
of you
that made me feel
like i was someone
worth loving
what happened to us

childlike treatment.

tired of being treated
like a child
instead of your partner
this used to be fun
i used to feel wanted
now i question
my own self worth
while trying to hold on
to you

fight then leave.

watching my parents fight
then leave each other
taught me every argument
brings my relationship closer
to its end

insane.

never lose your mind
over someone who
rarely thinks about you

giving.

give me loyalty

give me truth

give me adventure

give me you

process.

tell her

show her

repeat

on this day.

today is your stepping-stone
toward the life
you deserve

weak foundation.

love built on any lie
will crumble

you, muse.

and you're the girl
poets love to write about

better.

changed behavior
is the only way
to say i'm sorry

any year.

this year
drained me dry
this year
was the hardest
of my life

no, never.

never lose sleep
over someone
who isn't afraid
to lose you

dark side.

we hide our sadness
in the darkness
near the moon

a good night.

good night
doesn't come easy
most nights are hard

minimalist.

your love, unkind

truly mad.

the madness

in being afraid of love

but wanting to be loved

single black female.

i am a product

of a single black female

who was overlooked

and taken for granted

i am the result of a woman

learning to conquer

and triumph on her own

by herself

nothing is impossible

all the years.

i woke up this morning

wanting to call you

but i couldn't

i no longer have your number

and even if i did

you wouldn't have answered

the years have turned us

into strangers

or more like enemies

below earth.

and sometimes relationships
become caskets made of wood
buried 6 feet beneath
the surface of the earth
the saddest part is that
we were still breathing
barely alive
holding on to the death
of whatever we thought
this was

3 hours ago.

she will love

she will stay

she will fight

and she will leave

if you refuse

to match her effort

good women get tired

of bad treatment

much stronger.

they can't break the woman
who has built her strength
on the pain she's experienced

3:25 a.m.

the sadness

is what keeps me awake

at night

the sadness is what makes

me restless

the fighter.

alone

tired

broken

afraid

but she kept fighting

11:11 before midnight.

what she wanted

was a man

not a child

someone who would

make an effort

everything should never

fall on the shoulders

of a woman

awake alone.

i woke up alone
this morning
this was nothing new
i bring someone home
and they never stay
either they offer up
some excuse to leave
or i forbid them
to remain lying next to me
i hate this deadly cycle
of bringing home strangers
because every morning
i fear looking into the mirror
at my own judging eyes
unable to recognize my own reflection
i then become a stranger
to myself
the more i wake up alone

love of damnation.

drowning in forbidden waters

we ignore the warning signs

color blind to the red flags

deaf to the sounds of chaos

fighting for nothing

staying without reason

trying to force love

while accepting hatred

calling it love

while being content with pain

mistaken for love.

i misplaced my interest

by investing my energy

into you

lies we believe.

death sits on the tongues
of liars
reciting their version
of love
acting out empathy
like a bad improvisation
of someone who cares
and we believe it
because we're alone
filling that void
with a lie of a relationship

winter fills me.

winter lives within me
summer, no longer in my reach
my heart is frozen
i no longer shiver in the cold

12.19.16.

love yourself
so that you can love someone
who will love you just as much

some insight.

your relationship has become
a drought
you find yourself reaching
for something that your partner
is no longer willing to give
you, full of love
they are now empty
it's time to move forward
with your life left behind.
whatever or whoever hurt you
leave it and them behind you

under the rubble.

i'm still trying
to find myself
under the crumbling foundation
of everything we were

artists in suffering.

inspired by sadness

my writer's block is joy

our protest.

poetry is protest

against pain and heartache

the misery.

miserable people

need others to feel misery

in order to feel less miserable

the restlessness.

the real enemy
is the restlessness
you feel at 3 a.m.

cosmic.

you are madness

and magic

covered with skin

the universe lives

within your eyes

a cosmic power

surging through your bones

01.01.14.

loneliness

was sitting next to you

covered in scars

caused by your betrayal

beneath below.

we bury sadness
beneath fake smiles
and forced laughter
afraid of our own
emotional truth

lying eyes.

love will make you hallucinate

a truth that is really a lie

current.

social media

destroyed the social life

emojis have crippled the alphabet

<u>rem.</u>

lucid dreaming

of peace

the only place i find joy

is in my dreams

when i'm asleep

forcing my hand.

be the person you promise
to become after every argument
give me the love
you claim to have
whenever you're sorry
i can't keep going back
to a place that brings me harm
i refuse to hold on
while you force me to let go

shine through.

while they look at you

and see a broken woman

under the moon

i see a star shining in darkness

i see a soul that keeps the sky lit

i heard you.

some whispers are strong enough

to destroy the heart

some whispers are loud enough

to shatter the soul

the harshest things live within

the walls of a whisper

ticking away.

overthinking is a bomb
ticking away in the mind

inhale. exhale.

breathe
collect the air
of what you desire
and breathe out
what doesn't belong

no spare.

with one life

no spares

i choose to live

even if it means

moving forward without you

the heart wants.

if you want love
you have to loosen your grip
on the person incapable
of caring for your heart

whiskey on my tongue.

lies on lucifer's lips

my heart in the hands of god

my eyes on my future

my hands gripping my past

i'd like to move on

but it's a struggle letting go

my truth hidden in these words

the pain residing in my soul

i scream silently

my sadness hidden beneath my smile

i've been missing my peace of mind

and the innocence i had as a child

god grant me serenity

my heart cries for something more

i fear that if i talk to god

with whiskey on my breath

i'll get ignored

darkest part of love.

black butterflies

perched upon black roses

underneath black clouds

blending with black smoke

my heart is uneasy

burdened by restlessness

my mind screams

creating a sound of silence

silenced by my ability to pretend

to be okay

never loud enough for others

to hear

overwhelmed with fear

i'm afraid of love

still putting out the flames

the fire left behind

the one without a name

the one i'm trying to forget

the one who forgot about me

i can't breathe

i can't see

i can't speak

i can't hear

when love feels like death

deceptively lucid.

strangely

i'm unable to tell

my dreams apart from reality

struggling with the thought

that all good things

are just creations of my mind

the things i desire

the things i wish for

what if my eyes are closed

what if they've been closed

all this time

only to be awakened to a reality

filled with everything i've been

running from

written in darkness.

nothingness fills our room

consumed by our own brokenness

undone by tainted love

we were never supposed

to survive this

i'm learning to accept this truth

9 ft under.

we fall into pits
labeled love
we hold on to a love
that feels like hell
fanning the flames
with the lies
we tell ourselves
pretending to know romance
while only familiar
with pain steps

use their lies
as stepping stones
toward the truth
you deserve

too much to settle.

my fun is too big

for clubs

my ambition is too big

for a job i hate

my love is too big

for an unhealthy relationship

shady sight.

through rose-colored glasses

hate looks like love

casino.

relationships, like slot machines
we make foolish gambles
even though the odds are against us

writer's block.

there are no words
to describe the pain
my heart struggles
to spell out

tragic.

the greatest tragedy in life
is not living peacefully

false friendship.

most of my friends
were just enemies
wearing smiles

safe deception.

we've come to believe liars
because the truth hurts

loose shoestrings.

i tripped over your lies
and fell in love
with the person
you pretended to be

say no more.

sometimes saying no
means saying yes
to something better
down the line

main issue.

the problem is
you'd rather wait
for him to treat you right
instead of preserving yourself
for someone willing and ready
to love you correctly

almost there 722.

i kiss the clouds

with you beside me

first class

thousands of feet above

the ground

overlooking everything

from my window seat

hand in hand

with my lover

the time is now 7:22 p.m.

2 more hours until we land

half life.

you've been living
a half life
surrounded by half truths
half of you buried
the rest, struggling to survive
it's time to find
yourself again
it's time to live

cold and alone.

i'm cold

despite it being summer

i'm alone

despite being taken

under internally.

life jackets don't work
when you're drowning
from within

leave them.

if you want love
you have to leave behind
the people who encourage you
to hate yourself

lucid oasis.

sleeping the pain away
sometimes the only way
to escape the nightmare
is to dream

no fighting alone.

some relationships

are war zones

most love is a battle

some are fighting to win

some are fighting to survive

regardless of it all

you should never

be fighting alone

and still my champion.

in 48 seconds
i watched fans
become enemies
the same ones cheering
now silenced by defeat
the same ones ever so supportive
now throwing piles of insults
leaving negative comments
under photos via social media
demeaning the name
of their former hero
in 48 seconds i watched
your world crumble around you
and even though you lost
you were still my champion

<u>everyone.</u>

flirting with love
but you decide
to accept pain

river of tears.

cry

drown your devils

with the tears they caused

swim to shore

from the rivers you've made

gone again.

and just like that
happiness escapes me
like rain during a drought

all documented.

i will fill these pages
with documentation
of all the times
you caused me pain
with little black letters
paper as the canvas
my art will scream out
the many ways you hurt me

never I.

you shouldn't have to beg
for what you deserve
you shouldn't have to fight for
someone who refuses to fight for you

one year.

a year changes so much

one year later

and i still don't recognize

my own reflection

a year later

and things will never be the same

but maybe that's a good thing

you settle.

the relationship you settle for
becomes the hell you live in

rare woman.

love her entirely

give her everything

she deserves

acknowledge her very existence

as the greatest moment in your life

understand that she is a rare

occurrence, a life-changing event

and never let her go

for if you should lose her

you would have lost

the most precious thing on this earth

never II.

notice the way her eyes
light up at the first sight of you
understand the joy that fills
her chest when she thinks of you
and never make her regret
falling in love with you
for most women
falling head over heels
takes courage
never punish the woman
who is brave enough
to open her heart to you

written here.

instead of holding on
to all the pain in my heart
i chose to write about it
i took the lies served to me as truth
and poured it all out
on pages that are now bound together
held in place by a cover
that bears my name
witness my anguish in every word
the errors of my past
the mistakes i've learned from
all written here and put on display
with hopes of helping others
who know my pain

my struggle is yours.

sometimes i struggle with the idea
of someone loving me completely
sometimes i fear that i may not
love myself enough
too much of me has been wasted
pretending to be happy
content with my own damnation
content with the hell that i built
on lies of love
and this need to fill my own void
of loneliness

i struggle with the future
my past overshadowed
by all the toxic relationships
that led to heartache
and even though the present
should be a gift

in this moment

i struggle with hope

for hope has often been

the enemy

and everything i hoped for

has often gone up in flames

turning my dreams into ashes

but this is my struggle

and this is my story

you, the muse.

this one is for the young woman
reading this right now
searching for hope in these words
searching for her own strength
in this book
this one is for the young woman
who feels like giving in or giving up
the young woman who has fallen victim
to a love that was a lie
or a man who was a dog
or a relationship that turned out
to be a version of hell
she never deserved

this one is for the young woman

who searches for peace

in the words of a poet

who is still trying to run away

from chaos

this one is for the young woman

who finds clarity

in the art that i've created

these words are for the young woman

who at her age

should never know heartbreak

but she does and i'm here

to do whatever it is that i can do

to make things a little easier

this one is for the young woman

with tears in her eyes

as she reads these words

tired, restless, fatigued emotionally

this was inspired by you

where magic lives.

gifts given without

expecting anything in return

genuine compliments

without anything else attached to them

unconditional love

not broken by anger

or overshadowed by hate

these are the things

you deserve

these are the things

you should hold out for

no more settling for a love
that hurts or feels like hell
no more exchanging yourself
for the company of someone
who'd rather use you

magic lives within every part of you
the type of magic that most men
won't understand
the type of magic that most men
will never appreciate
and that's completely fine
because you, my dear,
are not for everyone
and you, my dear,
are one of a kind

invisible.

i wear the names

of my abusers

on my skin in invisible ink

but even while no one notices

it still hurts

deep under my skin

where their hands once touched me

bruises unseen by others

my smile has become a distraction

oftentimes i use happiness

to conceal the chaos

that has plagued my life

games.

i was asking you
to give me more
than you originally intended
promises made with your fingers
crossed behind your back
smiling in my face
plotting in my absence
this was all a game
and i played it
with my eyes closed

where gardens never grow.

out of loneliness
we hold on to people
who make us feel lonely
knowing nothing but pain
we choose toxic relationships
because of familiarity
we're used to being lied to
and so the truth isn't expected
hatred disguises itself as love
so much, that we've tricked ourselves
into believing that being in love
must destroy us
and anything of less drama
is somehow too boring
or at the surface, just too good
for us
we mistake fighting and yelling
for passion

we accept chaos

while begging for peace

we expect to be handed roses

by the same hands

of our abusers

we sit and wait for kind words

from the lips of those

who choose to destroy

our hearts verbally

we wait too long

for the love we desire

we wait too long

for a love that continues

to escape us

because we're afraid

to step outside of our comfort zone

we plant our seeds of hope

in ditches that measure 6 feet

beneath the ground

waiting for flowers to bloom

in dead soil

waiting for gardens to grow

in the mud of despair . . .

index.

planting gardens in graves II

copyright © 2018 by r.h. Sin. All rights
reserved. Printed in the United States of
America. No part of this book may be used or
reproduced in any manner whatsoever without
written permission except in the case of
reprints in the context of reviews.

Andrews McMeel Publishing
a division of Andrews McMeel Universal
1130 Walnut Street, Kansas City, Missouri 64106

www.andrewsmcmeel.com

18 19 20 21 22 RR2 10 9 8 7 6 5 4 3 2 1

ISBN: 978-1-4494-8762-1

Library of Congress Control Number: 2017950152

Editor: Patty Rice

Art Director, Designer: Diane Marsh

Production Editor: David Shaw

Production Manager: Cliff Koehler

attention: schools and businesses

Andrews McMeel books are available at
quantity discounts with bulk purchase for
educational, business, or sales promotional
use. For information, please e-mail the Andrews
McMeel Publishing Special Sales Department:
specialsales@amuniversal.com.